SAVING WILDLIFE

Woodland and Forest Animals

Sonya Newland

W
FRANKLIN WATTS
LONDON • SYDNEY

This edition 2014

First published in 2010 by
Franklin Watts
338 Euston Road
London NW1 3BH

Franklin Watts Australia
Level 17/207 Kent Street
Sydney NSW 2000

Produced for Franklin Watts by
White-Thomson Publishing
+44 (0)843 208 7460
www.wtpub.co.uk

Series consultant: Sally Morgan
Designer: Clare Nicholas
Picture researcher: Amy Sparks

A CIP catalogue record for this book is available from the British Library.

ISBN (pb): 978 1 4451 2984 6
ISBN (Library ebook): 978 1 4451 2222 9

Dewey Classification: 591.7'3

Picture Credits
Dreamstime: Cover (Ekaterina Dushenina), 5 (Michael Woodruff), 6 (Kelly Boreson), 7 (Calamityjohn), 8 (Outdoorsman), 9t (Oksanaphoto), 11t (Angel Sosa), 13b (James Hearn), 15 (Viktor Glupov), 18l (Eric Issele), 21 (Jason Kasomovic), 22l (Darren Green), 24t (Paulo Simão); **Nature Photo Library:** 9b (Pete Oxford), 11b (Yuri Shibney), 13t (Shattil & Rozinski), 20b (Dave Watts), 22r (Pete Oxford), 26b (John Downer); **iStock:** 23t (Clint Spencer); **NHPA:** 19t (A.N.T. Photo Library); **Photolibrary:** 12 (Christina Krutz), 14 (Helge Schulz), 17b (Bildagentur RM), 20t (Peter Weimann), 23b (Allen Blake Sheldon), 25b (Bill Beatty), 27t (Jared Hobbs), 27b (Maurice Tibbles); **Shutterstock:** 10 (Tom Tietz), 16 (Wendy Nero), 17t (Susan Flashman), 18r (Bruce MacQueen), 19b (Jo Chambers), 24b (Charles Shapiro), 26t (RJ08).

Every attempt has been made to clear copyright. Should there be any inadvertent omission please apply to the publisher for rectification.

Printed in China

Franklin Watts is a division of Hachette Children's Books, an Hachette UK Company.
www.hachette.co.uk

Contents

Words in **bold** are in the glossary on page 31.

Woodland and Forest Habitats

Woodlands and forests are places where trees are the main type of plant. They can be found all over the world except in Antarctica and most of the Arctic, in deserts, grasslands and on the very tops of mountains.

What is a forest?

In forests, the trees are very close together. Forests are often dark because the branches and leaves form a kind of 'roof' that lets in very little sunlight. Woodlands are lighter because the trees are further apart. Sometimes there are **clearings** in woods, where no trees grow and sunlight can reach the ground.

Forest types

There are three main types of forest – tropical, temperate and boreal. Tropical forests, often called rainforests, are found in the warmest parts of the world, near the **Equator**. Temperate forests grow in cooler regions. There are different types of temperate forest, including rainforest, but most have trees that lose their leaves in autumn and winter. Boreal forests grow in very cold **climates** and are usually made up of evergreen trees. This book looks at animals that live in the world's temperate and boreal forests.

Black bear
(page 8)

North America

Salamander
(page 23)

South America

Woodland wildlife

Rainforests are home to more types of animals and plants than anywhere on Earth, but thousands of species live in temperate and boreal forests and woodlands. Creatures as small as ants and as large as bears feast on flowers, fruit, insects or smaller animals. In the cold winter months some **hibernate** while others **migrate** to warmer parts of the world.

▼ *Forests can be found in most parts of the world. Close to the Equator are tropical forests. Temperate and boreal forests lie in cooler northern regions.*

Raccoon dog (page 12)

Temperate forest

Boreal forest

Rainforest

Europe

Asia

Africa

Tropic of Cancer

Equator

Australia

Tropic of Capricorn

Tasmanian devil (page 17)

Iberian lynx (page 11)

5

Forests Under Threat

People have always cut down trees, but recently this has been happening on a much larger scale and more rapidly than ever before.

Natural dangers

Some natural events have caused forests to disappear. **Wildfires** can sweep through forests, burning trees and plants and killing animals. Fierce storms can blow down the trees. Insect invasions can kill off plants that other animals rely on for food. However, **conservationists** have learned that sometimes fires can be good for forests, clearing away dead plants and making way for new ones to grow. Sometimes putting out fires can be more harmful than leaving them to burn.

Human threats

People are also threatening forest wildlife. They cut down trees to use the wood and so that they can farm or live in the once-forested areas. The animals lose their homes and food supply, and are forced to live in smaller and smaller areas. Sometimes animals are hunted for food or their fur, or they are killed by local people protecting their crops. Cutting down trees also contributes to **climate change**.

▼ *Large areas of forest are cut down so that the timber can be sold.*

Web of life

Everything in forest **habitats** relies on other living things to survive. Creatures such as earthworms help keep the soil healthy so plants can grow, providing food and shelter for wildlife. Insects such as butterflies and bees **pollinate** flowers. Small **mammals** and birds eat insects, and larger mammals eat smaller ones. This means that any changes can affect everything that lives there, so it is important to preserve this precious environment.

▶ *All woodland creatures rely on others – as a source of food or to keep the soil, flowers and trees healthy. This American Robin has caught a worm to feed his chicks.*

ENDANGERED ANIMALS

The International Union for the Conservation of Nature (IUCN) – see page 28 – lists animals according to how endangered they are.

Extinct: Died out completely.

Extinct in the wild: Only survive in captivity.

Critically **endangered**: Extremely high risk of becoming extinct in the near future.

Endangered: High risk of becoming extinct in the wild.

Vulnerable: High risk of becoming endangered in the wild.

Near threatened: Likely to become endangered in the near future.

Least concern: Lowest risk of becoming endangered.

Big Bears

Bears thrive in temperate forests. Their dark fur provides camouflage, and their thick coats protect them in winter. Bears will eat almost anything they can find in the forest, from acorns to animals as large as deer.

Black bears

American black bears can be found in different habitats in North America – from mountains to open landscapes – but they prefer forests. They are good at climbing, so they can reach food that grows or lives high up in the trees. Black bears are not considered endangered, but because they are hunted for sport their numbers are carefully monitored to make sure that not too many are being killed.

Brown bears

Brown bears once roamed all over Europe and Asia, but not many survive on these **continents**, and in Europe brown bears are a **protected species**. The grizzly bear, a type of brown bear, is only found in North America. Many live in **national parks**, so they are safe from human threats, but others are suffering because of **deforestation** and hunting. The US Fish and Wildlife Service is trying to increase the numbers of grizzly bears by breeding them in captivity and then releasing them to areas where there are not many left.

◄ *Black bears are protected by an international **trade agreement** that tries to stop illegal **poaching**.*

EXTREME ANIMALS

Grizzly bears can kill an animal or a human with a single swipe from their large paws.

▲ Grizzly bears wade into rivers and catch fish with their sharp claws.

SAVING WILDLIFE

Sloth bear

Sloth bears of the **deciduous** forests of Asia are hunted or caught and forced to 'dance' for entertainment. The World Society for the Protection of Animals (WSPA) is working with the Wildlife Trust of India (WTI) to stop these practices. They run public-education programmes, rescue mistreated bears and try to prevent illegal poaching.

Cats on the Prowl

Forests are the perfect habitat for big cats – they can climb well and move easily through the trees. Their patterned fur offers good camouflage so they can sneak up on their prey.

Forest felines

Cats such as tigers and jaguars live in steamy rainforests, but many other types of cat – including bobcats, lynx, puma and some types of leopard – prefer cooler climates. Many cats are hunted for their fur, or are killed because they attack **livestock** or simply because people are afraid of them.

▼ *North American bobcats adapt easily to different habitats, so they are not considered endangered.*

With fewer than 150 left in the wild in Spain, the Iberian lynx is one of the world's most endangered cats.

Lynx on the brink

One cat that has not survived hunting and habitat loss is the Iberian lynx, whose numbers in the wild have fallen to under 150. WWF (see page 28) is working with the Spanish government on a **captive-breeding** programme. If this is successful, the lynx will later be released into the wild, saving the **species** from extinction.

SAVING WILDLIFE

Amur leopard

There are 30–35 Amur leopards left in Russia and China. The Amur Leopard and Tiger Alliance (ALTA) is working to save these cats by stopping illegal poaching, educating local people and protecting the leopard's habitat. **Conservation** programmes have already saved the Amur tiger, so there is hope for this endangered leopard.

WHAT DO YOU THINK?

To help save the Amur leopard where it is most at risk, the ALTA (see left) pay local farmers compensation if a leopard kills their animals. Do you think it's right to pay people not to kill endangered species, and why?

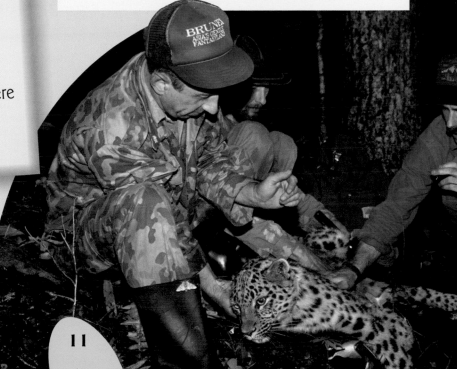

Researchers in Russia attach a special collar to an Amur leopard so they can track it in the wild.

Wild Dogs

Trees provide good cover for wild dogs such as wolves, jackals and foxes. Although they are not good climbers, there are plenty of animals on the ground for the dogs to hunt.

Protecting raccoon dogs

Although not yet considered endangered, the raccoon dog of Asia may soon be threatened because it is widely hunted for its fur, meat and bones – especially in Japan. An island in Japan is now a protected area, set aside especially for these wild dogs. There are also now some raccoon dogs in northern Europe and parts of Russia.

▼ *Raccoon dogs are hunted in China and Japan so their fur can be made into clothing.*

This red wolf is in Victoria Zoo in the USA. Two-thirds of the remaining red wolves are in captivity.

Dholes in danger

Dholes are a rare species of Asian wild dog. They once ranged right across Asia, but deforestation has put them in danger. Animals that the dholes rely on for food, such as deer and wild pigs, move to other areas so the dogs are losing both their homes and their food supply. The Dhole Conservation Project is raising awareness about this little-known dog, and it is a protected species.

EXTREME ANIMALS

While many animals became extinct at the end of the last ice age around 10,000 years ago, wolves survived and have been roaming Earth for more than a million years.

On the Hoof

Many types of deer and other hoofed animals once lived in the world's forests and woodlands. Although some have suffered from habitat loss and hunting, they are still found on almost every continent.

▼ *Male red deer are big animals, but they are still threatened by hunters, especially humans, who value their antlers.*

Natural prey

Deer are hunted by many different forest animals, including big cats, bears and wolves. They are sometimes even snatched by birds of prey. However, they are also popular targets for human hunters, who kill them for sport. As their woodland homes have been cut down, most deer have adapted to living in more open areas. Although this means they can survive habitat loss, it does make them easier prey for both animal and human **predators**.

Red-deer management

Although most deer species are not under threat, many experts think that they might be in the near future because of deforestation. To stop this happening, several countries have conservation programmes. In the UK, the Forestry Commission works with local people to manage deer populations, and in Greece WWF monitors the small population of red deer in the Parnitha National Park. This is especially important as the area suffered damage from wildfire in 2007.

Medium Mammals

As well as bears, cats and wild dogs, several other hunters make their homes in forests and woodlands, including wild pigs, wolverines and martens.

◀ *Wolverines look like small bears, but they are actually members of the weasel family.*

Big weasels

Wolverines live in northern boreal forests, where they feast on smaller mammals such as squirrels and rabbits. Suffering from habitat loss, hunting and slow breeding, the number of wolverines has dropped dramatically in the past 100 years, especially in the USA. Environmental groups are campaigning to make wolverines an endangered species so they will be protected by law.

SAVING WILDLIFE

Tasmanian devil
Since the mid-1990s, the greatest threat to the Tasmanian devil has been a disease called devil facial tumour. Currently only found on the Australian island of Tasmania, these **marsupials** are being bred in zoos on mainland Australia so they can be released into the wild there.

Running wild

Wild boar thrive in woodlands because they will eat almost anything – from nuts and berries to small deer. In turn they are preyed on by larger **carnivores**. They were hunted to extinction in many parts of Europe, but now some countries have reintroduced wild boars from other countries with great success.

WHAT DO YOU THINK?

The rapid increase in wild boars in Germany has caused problems, as the animals damage property and have even dug up graves. How could populations of animals like this be controlled? Should we be more careful when choosing which animals are reintroduced and why?

▲ *There are more than two million wild boar in Germany.*

Small Mammals

In the trees and in burrows on the ground, small mammals such as mice, rabbits, hedgehogs, skunks and chipmunks feast on the plentiful plants and insects of their forest habitat.

Abundant animals

Some woodland mammals are so abundant that they are considered pests, especially when they grow so bold that they move into urban areas. Others, including weasels and stoats, are deliberately killed to keep them under control. But all little woodland animals are affected by habitat loss and climate change, and when small mammals disappear, the larger animals that feed on them also suffer.

▼ *Woodland rabbits live in underground tunnels called warrens.*

EXTREME ANIMALS

American woodland skunks can spray their foul-smelling liquid with amazing accuracy as far as 3.5 m.

90 cm

SAVING WILDLIFE

Smoky mouse

The smoky mouse is found only in Australia, but the clearing of its forest home for timber and road building has made it an endangered species. The government of New South Wales has begun a recovery programme, which includes protecting the areas where smoky mice still live, controlling the numbers of animals that prey on them and educating local people about how they can help save the mice.

Save the squirrel

Red squirrels are **native** to Europe, and there are still lots of them in many countries. In the UK they are being wiped out by grey squirrels, introduced from America. There are now only 140,000 red squirrels – a small number compared to the 2.5 million greys. The Forestry Commission is researching ways to increase the numbers of red squirrels. The Save Our Squirrels campaign is also encouraging the public to help by reporting sightings of red squirrels to monitor populations.

▶ *In countries such as Finland and Russia, red squirrels are threatened by people hunting them for their fur.*

By the Water

Along the edges of woodland rivers and streams live a variety of water-loving mammals. They often build their burrows in the riverbanks and feed on fish.

Otters on the water

Otters live by the water but use nearby woodlands for breeding and **foraging** for food. In Europe and North America, water **pollution** and the destruction of woodlands have placed them under threat. They are a now a protected species and are bred in special otter **sanctuaries** in many countries.

◀ *Water pollution is a big threat to otters and other riverbank creatures.*

SAVING WILDLIFE

Platypus
The curious-looking platypus of Australia's forests was saved from extinction in the early twentieth century by laws that banned their hunting. Although there are lots of platypuses now, experts are concerned that pollution and habitat loss might pose new threats.

Endangered voles

Although plentiful across Europe and America, water voles are among the most threatened woodland mammals in the UK. This is partly because pollution has **contaminated** their habitat, but also because American minks have been introduced to the UK, and these larger creatures prey on water voles. In 2008, the British government said that water voles would be fully protected by law.

Beaver builders

Beavers are very important to the woodland **ecosystem**. They are famous for gnawing down trees to build dams. This creates pools of water for them to live by, and which other species use as vital water sources. It also helps make room for fresh young trees to grow. Beavers were nearly extinct in some parts of Europe only 10 years ago, but people now recognise the important role they play in their habitat. They are protected by international trade laws and are not considered endangered any longer.

EXTREME ANIMALS

Once beavers start building a dam, they won't stop until they have finished. The largest beaver dam ever recorded was 1.5 km long.

Slimy and Scaly Creatures

Reptiles and amphibians are at home in shady woodlands and forests. The damp ground, pools and abundant insects for food are all vital for the survival of these creatures.

Cool snakes

Although many snakes live in warm tropical regions, some of them prefer the cooler climate of northern forests. The black rat snake of North America preys on rabbits and rodents on the forest floor, but it can slither up trees where its dark skin helps it blend in among the branches. The timber rattlesnake, found in the USA's deciduous forests, is one of the most dangerous snakes in the country. One bite can kill a human.

◀ *Timber rattlesnakes are declining in number and are the subject of conservation efforts by the Endangered and Nongame Species Program in the USA.*

SAVING WILDLIFE

Angonoka tortoise
Once thriving in Madagascar's dry forests, the Angonoka tortoise is now listed as critically endangered. However, thanks to recent captive-breeding programmes and careful management of their forest habitat, they are being saved from extinction. They continue to be at great risk though because of the illegal pet trade.

Pond life

Salamanders, frogs and turtles are all at home in damp woodland environments. They usually live near pools and feed on insects on the forest floor. Among the most threatened **reptiles** are American box turtles. They are often caught as pets, but a bigger problem is **fragmentation** – when areas of forest are cut down, separating groups of animals.

▲ *As they try to get from one part of the forest to the other, many box turtles are run down by cars.*

WHAT DO YOU THINK?

One of the main threats to box turtles is climate change, and some people have said this is a good argument for keeping them in captivity, where their environment can be controlled. What are the arguments for and against keeping box turtles as pets?

◀ *The northern red salamander lives in deciduous forests in the US states of Ohio and Indiana (where it is listed as endangered).*

Minibeasts

Insects and other bugs play a vital role in the woodland ecosystem. There are so many species, however, that experts think there may be insects under threat that we don't even know about.

Insects everywhere

On the forest floor, snails, worms, centipedes, ants, beetles and many other minibeasts live among the decaying leaves, moss and fallen trees. Worms help keep the soil healthy by creating tunnels that allow air and water to seep into it. Butterflies and bees carry pollen between flowers, which is important for seed production. Some insects even control other insect populations, such as caterpillars, which eat plant leaves.

▲ *Too many caterpillars in a forest can cause problems because they eat the leaves of plants.*

EXTREME ANIMALS

Monarch butterflies make one of the longest insect migrations in the world to and from their wintering grounds in Mexican forests. They travel up to 4,500 km every year.

Spruce-fir moss spider

Tiny spruce-fir moss spiders live in fir forests in the USA, but they are being wiped out by an insect invasion from Europe. Balsam-wooly adelgids are killing off the fir trees, which exposes the moss in which the spiders live, causing them to dry out and die. Little is known about these spiders but research is helping experts understand more, and captive-breeding programmes have begun.

The forest food chain

Insects are eaten by birds, small mammals, reptiles and **amphibians**. If the numbers of insects drop, the survival of larger animals is threatened. In turn, even bigger animals come under threat because they feed on the insect-eaters. Conserving woodlands and forests will make sure these important creatures survive.

▼ *An American toad feasts on a large insect called a cicada.*

Birds and Bats

Woodlands are alive with the sound of songbirds in the branches. Owls nest in the tree trunks and woodpeckers tap out insects. High above the treetops, birds of prey circle in search of food.

Songbirds

Songbirds all over the world are being affected by habitat loss and fragmentation. Some of them need quite large areas in which to nest and breed, so when their homes are broken up by roads and houses they are unable to breed successfully and their numbers decline.

◀ *Songbirds such as blue jays are not currently endangered, but some may come under threat as more woodland areas are destroyed.*

SAVING WILDLIFE

American bald eagle

The recovery of the American bald eagle is one of the greatest success stories. The use of the **pesticide** DDT almost killed them off, because it got into water supplies and poisoned the fish that the eagles ate. By the mid-twentieth century there were only 417 pairs left. A huge clean-up operation helped reverse the damage. There are now more than 50,000 pairs.

EXTREME ANIMALS

The endangered bumblebee bat is one of the smallest mammals on Earth – some are no bigger than a thumb.

3 cm

Keeping bats safe

Because they are sensitive to light and heat, bats are usually found roosting in cool, shady woodland areas. Many bat species are endangered and some are protected species in Europe and America, which means it is illegal to kill or injure a bat.

Night flyers

Most owls are **nocturnal** creatures, nesting in trees or burrows in the ground. Groups try to protect woodland to save endangered owls such as spotted and masked owls.

◄ *Owls such as this spotted owl use their colouring to blend into the background during the day.*

What Can We Do?

More and more forests and woodlands are being cut down every year, but people are more aware than ever before of how important it is to protect these precious environments. Sometimes national governments take steps to protect their endangered creatures. International organisations work with local communities to make a difference. But even individuals can help save woodland wildlife.

Find out more...

WWF (www.wwf.org.uk)
This is the UK site of the largest international animal conservation organisation. On this site you can follow links to information on all sorts of endangered animals and find out what WWF is doing to save woodland and forest creatures.

EDGE of Existence (www.edgeofexistence.org)
The EDGE of Existence is a special global conservation programme that focuses on saving what it calls evolutionary distinct and globally endangered (EDGE) species – unusual animals and plants that are under threat.

International Union for Conservation of Nature (www.iucn.org)
The IUCN produces the Red List, which lists all the world's known endangered species and classifies them by how under threat they are. You can see the whole list of endangered animals on the website, as well as discover what the IUCN does to address environmental issues all over the world.

Convention on International Trade in Endangered Species (www.cites.org)
CITES is an international agreement between governments that aims to ensure trade in wild animal species does not threaten their survival. It lists animals that are considered to be under threat from international trading, and makes laws accordingly.

US Fish and Wildlife Service (www.fws.gov)
This government organisation was set up to manage and preserve wildlife in the USA. It helps manage wildlife reserves and makes sure laws that protect endangered animals are properly enforced.

World Society for the Protection of Animals (www.wspa.org.uk)
The WSPA is an animal-welfare organisation with international campaigns to draw attention to and stamp out cruelty to animals, including exploiting creatures such as sloth bears for entertainment.

Forestry Commission (www.forestry.gov.uk)
The UK Forestry Commission manages the country's woodland and forests, planting trees and protecting forest and woodland wildlife.

Do more...

Protect local woodland

Find out what is being done to protect and conserve your local woodland and the animals that live there, and offer your support. Simply going along and collecting litter can help keep this environment safe for wildlife.

Sign a petition

Petitions are documents asking governments or organisations to take action on something people are concerned about. Some of the organisations on page 28 have online petitions that you can sign to show your support for their campaigns.

Celebrate World Forestry Day

World Forestry Day is celebrated every year on 21 March. With your friends or your class, organise an event to mark the day.

Go to the zoo

Find out if your local zoo is involved in any captive-breeding programmes and go along to find out more. Just visiting the zoo helps support these programmes.

Adopt an animal

For a small contribution to some conservation organisations you get to 'adopt' a woodland or forest animal. They will send you information about your adopted animal and keep you up to date on all the conservation efforts in the area.

Read more...

This is My Planet
by Jan Thornhill
(Franklin Watts, 2012)

Animal Kingdom (The World of Infographics) by Jon Richards and Ed Simkins (Wayland, 2013)

Saving Wildlife (Eco Alert) by Rebecca Hunter (Franklin Watts, 2012)

Very Wonderful, Very Rare – Saving the Most Endangered Wildlife on Earth by Baillie and Butcher (Franklin Watts, 2013)

Every effort has been made by the publisher to ensure that these websites contain no inappropriate or offensive material. However, because of the nature of the Internet, it is impossible to guarantee that the content of these sites will not be altered. We strongly advise that Internet access is supervised by a responsible adult.

Woodland and Forest Animals Quiz

See how much you can remember about woodland and forest animals by taking the quiz below. Look back through the book to find the answers if you need to. The answers are on page 32.

1. What are the three main types of forest?

2. What natural events can destroy forest and woodland habitats?

3. Why are people cutting down forests?

4. Why are sloth bears under threat?

5. Which brown bear is being reintroduced by the US Fish and Wildlife Service?

6. In which country do the only remaining Iberian lynx survive?

7. How is the ALTA trying to save the Amur leopard?

8. What animals do dholes eat?

9. Which country has a special island reserve for raccoon dogs?

10. How many red wolves are left in the wild?

11. What is another name for the European bison?

12. What natural disaster affected the Parnitha National Park in Greece in 2007?

13. What animal family do wolverines belong to?

14. Which disease is killing off large numbers of Tasmanian devils?

15. How many red squirrels are left in the UK?

16. Which introduced animal is threatening the survival of water voles in the UK?

17. In which country can you find platypuses?

18. Where is the only place that Angonoka tortoises survive?

19. Which pesticide almost caused the extinction of the bald eagle?

20. Which bat is about the size of a thumb?

Glossary

amphibians cold-blooded animals that spend some of their time on land and some in water.

camouflage the colour or patterns on an animal that help it blend in with its surroundings.

captive breeding when endangered animals are specially bred in zoos or wildlife reserves so that they can then be released back into the wild.

carnivores animals that eat meat.

clearing an area in a wood where no trees grow so sunlight reaches the ground.

climate the regular pattern of temperature and weather conditions in a particular area.

climate change a difference in the expected weather conditions or temperatures across the world.

conservation preserving or managing habitats when they are under threat, have been damaged or destroyed.

conservationists people who work to protect the natural environment.

contaminated infected with harmful substances.

continents the Earth's seven great landmasses – Africa, Antarctica, Asia, Australia, Europe, North America and South America.

deciduous trees that shed their leaves in the autumn.

deforestation the cutting down of large areas of forest.

ecosystem all the different types of plants and animals that live in a particular area together with the non-living parts of the environment.

endangered at risk of becoming extinct.

Equator an imaginary line around the middle of the Earth that separates the world into the Northern and Southern hemispheres.

extinct when an entire species of animal has died out, so that there are none left on Earth.

foraging searching for food or other provisions such as material to build nests or burrows.

fragmentation the breaking up of areas of forest by cutting down the trees between them.

habitat the place where an animal lives.

hibernate to sleep or move around very little in winter.

livestock animals kept by people for meat or milk.

mammals warm-blooded animals that bear live young.

marsupial a mammal that nurtures its young in a pouch.

migrate to move from one place to another; many animals spend the summer in the Northern Hemisphere, but migrate south when the weather gets colder.

national parks special areas that are protected by national governments.

native an animal that occurs naturally in a particular country or region.

nocturnal coming out at night.

pesticide chemicals often used by farmers to keep insects off their crops.

poaching hunting an animal when it is against the law.

pollinate to transfer pollen from one flower to another, so that it can make seeds.

pollution spoiling the environment with man-made waste.

predator an animal that hunts others for food.

protected species animals or plants that are protected by law, so that it is illegal to do anything that threatens their survival.

reptiles cold-blooded animals that lay eggs and usually have scales or plates on their skin.

sanctuaries special places where animals that are endangered or injured are taken to help with conservation or to be treated.

species a type of animal or plant.

trade agreement an agreement between countries about whether certain things should be bought and sold.

wildfires naturally occurring fires that spread quickly.

Index

Numbers in **bold** indicate pictures

Quiz answers

1. Tropical, temperate and boreal; 2. Fires, storms and insect invasions; 3. To use the wood and to make way for houses and roads; 4. They are caught and used as 'dancing bears'; 5. Grizzly bear; 6. Spain; 7. Stopping illegal poaching, educating local people and protecting their habitat; 8. Deer and wild pigs; 9. Japan; 10. Around 100; 11. Wisent; 12. Wildfire; 13. Weasel; 14. Devil facial tumour; 15. 160,000; 16. Mink; 17. Australia; 18. Madagascar; 19. DDT; 20. Bumblebee bat